I0104159

Biography of a Name

Bill Rector

Published by Unsolicited Press

www.unsolicitedpress.com

info@unsolicitedpress.com

Copyright © 2018 Bill Rector

All Rights Reserved.

No part of this book may be reproduced or transmitted in any form or by any means without written permission from the publisher or author.

Unsolicited Press Books are distributed by Ingram.

Printed in the United States of America.

Attention schools and businesses: for discounted copies on large orders, please contact the publisher directly.

Editor: S.R. Stewart

Cover Design: UP Team

ISBN: 978-1-947021-34-1

Table of Contents

"To the best of my recollection, I must recall my memory, I cannot remember…"

Testimony of Jimmy Hoffa before the Senate Permanent Subcommittee on Investigations

The Missing Search

Jimmy Hoffa is buried
in this poem,
this small slice of
fiction not unlike a life.

As opposed to
the higher-ups who
hunted him we know
exactly where he lies.

There's a little Jimmy
Hoffa in all of us,
in the same way every
American embodies a

bit of Walt Whitman,
a scapula, let's say,
ditch digger's anchor
and oracle bone

given to the fire
by scholars who
dispute among themselves
how the writing breaks.

For his part, Jimmy
Hoffa has lent us
the third metacarpal
of his right hand,

the spine of any fist,
in this hard man
broken and healed
too many times.

The hole we are digging grows deeper with every word, which
ought to tell us something. It ought to tell us to put down the
shovel and call the FBI and tell them that Jimmy Hoffa is
seated across the table from us. And we would, but the lines
are busy. The G-men wouldn't come anyway. They know
where Jimmy Hoffa is. They've always known. They have an
eye in the sky and another in the earth and are watching us
even now, scribbling fresh reports as they file their stares
down to dust. Still

people surprise us
with their depths,
and the truth is Jimmy
Hoffa wouldn't be

caught dead in a form
of art with a smart
mouth that can't make
up its mind what it

should say or be about.
And we doubt
Hoffa knew much
of Whitman, although

Walt would have recognized
Hoffa among his roughs.
But the truth
isn't our concern.

Right now our concern
is how we're going
to pay the check
with a handful of lint.

Wrong Turn

Despite the jumble
his life became Jimmy
Hoffa has turned up not
a foot from our faces.
Corruption has left him
pure. Ink has seeped
back into his hair,
its natural pigment,
turning the roots
black again. Staring
back at us is the man
on the cover of *Life*
magazine in 1959. His
blunt brow and sharp
elbow protrude from the
driver's window of a fire
engine-red Peterbilt
semi-trailer truck.
He wears a white dress
shirt with silver cuff links
and a tie with a matching
stud. His glare fills the mirror,
as though he has his eye
on someone behind him,
that privileged runt

RFK, maybe, and a bunch
of government lawyers
from the Hoffa Task Force
shouting, What's the hold up?
See, Hoffa owned a demon
hotter than most,
with a pitchfork tongue
about to tell those around him,
every goddamn one,
especially those in power, Go to hell!
Or maybe there's more
to the man than that. Or
less. Looking through
the mirror into the past
his famous glower fades
to a reflective frown
and squint that masks

    fear. Uncertainty. Failing
    eyesight. On the run
    Hoffa always was,
    even as Teamster

        President, taking
        chances, veering in and out
        of his own blind spot
        like a scrappier Oedipus, back
        to the day he was born in Brazil,

Indiana. Yes, that Brazil,
that Indiana, where the sea
isn't even a memory but
fossils still have lives…

HOFFA MISSING

The famous Free
Press headline
could have been printed
when Hoffa was seven
years old and his father
died and his mother
moved the family
to Detroit or run off
the presses when he left
school to enter another,
harder one, or –

    Forget it.
    Can't you see
    Hoffa's puzzled?
    So many pieces
    of the life he lived
    are missing. Where
    the sky met the cornice
    of the tenement, the pigeon
    about to take wing before

the iceman's sawdust
-flecked boot, the boy,
frozen, looking
both ways before
crossing the street

forever... More
than anything Hoffa's
tired. He wants us
to explain why
he's been summoned
to face the world
again in this imagined

form, as if poetry confers
on its subject, if nothing
else, an eternal right

to ask, to know.
J. Edgar Hoover
smiles like a wound.
The song doesn't answer.
What song could?

Learning The Score

Ever wonder
what happened
to your hubcaps?
The rims with silver
spokes that appeared
to slow, reverse, and go
backward the faster
they spun? Were
they stolen? Did
they fly off
when you skidded
around the corner,
high on booze
and LSD, the double
axles of your eyes
suddenly big,
black and still?

Here's the funny part. (There's always a funny part.) Jimmy Hoffa was in the trunk of your Nova the whole time, curled like an aging fetus inside the spare. Remember? In that swollen era of chrome and innocence, the spare was as big as the other four tires, and you didn't need a college degree to find the lug wrench and put together the jack. You were young. You couldn't know that it would become your job to drive Hoffa to the compactor every day to be reborn as rumor and rebar to raise the Detroit Renaissance Center another floor, or that you'd go on working on the line, bent and dinged as a junkyard bumper, making the nation's vehicles ever more compact, until the day they roll off the conveyer belt six feet long, with a single door, never to open again?

A pig's eye?
A vat of lye?
A gravel pit?
The bedroom?
The kitchen?
The basement?
The beginning?
The middle?
The end?

Back to the Beginning

Flash! James R. "Jimmy" Hoffa has disappeared. He was reportedly last seen in the parking lot of the Red Fox Restaurant, where he'd arranged to meet certain underworld figures with Teamster ties. The car he left in was driven by Charles "Chuckie" O'Brien, whom Hoffa raised as a foster son after O'Brien's father died.

Want a tip?
Don't trust tips.
Hoffa's buried in
his brother William's
backyard gravel pit.
A grislier gag
renders Hoffa
last at a waste-fat
refinery in Wayne.
Here's a deeper
scoop: don't believe

a word you've read or heard. Jimmy Hoffa entered the Witness Protection Program at birth to keep from testifying against himself. Right now he's behind the wheel of a tractor trailer with a Teamster decal on I-40 near Nashville strumming a mile-long guitar with three slack strings and weathered fence posts for frets, singing as no one but Walt

Whitman has about America, about our barns and hills and factories and barrens and backyards with iron teeter-totters and cracked metal eggs where meat is grilled and dead cars, dead cars like the Buick Riviera that Charon drove from Bloomfield Township the night Jimmy disappeared, never missing a light, one finger on the wheel, invisible to the black and whites…

All these and none.
James Riddle Hoffa
now resides in
the middle of his
name, in iron,
concrete, crowd
noise, and silence
so complete you
can hear a pin
drop all the way
to the bottom
of Section 107
in the Meadow
-lands, where the
Giants have fallen
to the Steelers
in overtime.

Reservations

Jimmy Hoffa
and J. Edgar Hoover
go into a pub. The
place looks familiar.
It should. The bare,
swinging bulb above
the table casts shadows
that are, like history,
alternately large, then
small. *We are*
as much among the dead
as the living, muses Hoffa,
his thoughts flickering
between illumination
and despair, in synch
with the shrinking
arc of the filament.
Hoover brightens momentarily
with fame's incandescent
pallor. *A million*
things
flash through our minds then
none. Between one line
and the next their lives
become sparrow bones,

hieroglyphic girders,
half-alive neon,
man-high graffiti,
sirens' revolving prisms,
newsboy cries, streetcar bells,
lottery balls rattling
into a cage, pure sign
in other words,
like the flickering

V
A
C
A
N
C
Y

outside the Walt Whitman Hotel
in Camden, NJ, closed
since early last century
for remodeling. Hoffa bangs
the bell. He's rumpled. Tired.
He'd like a room. A meal.
Where's the clerk? The hop?
Hoffa's dressed as he was
the day he disappeared:

blue shirt, dark blue pants,
white socks, loafers.
The killers have been delayed.
The asphalt is hot.
It sticks to his soles.

The Society Page

MARBLEVILLE	PULP CITY	COAL TOWN
Everyone	What about you?	Between the town
Must go once	What about you?	I came from
If only to visit.	Where are you	And the one
To marvel at	Coming from	I've gone to
Those born	Is a question	Is the space
In niches.	Too often asked.	Where I now fit.
To riches.	A form of address	Follow the seam.
Chiseled.	In a conversation	A miner with
Polished.	Headed nowhere	No education
Placed upon	Fast. Your signs	Can tell you
Prancing horses.	Protest "War."	Coal is made of
Given a direction	Demand "No More-"	Living things.
And a horizon	Like a strike	Plant a shovel.
The lowborn	(strikes we know)	Pick a pick.
Never own.	With cloudy demands.	Coal's a living.
	Backbreaking demands.	Dad hacked
	But no workers.	Into his hands.
	Dig, Man?	They were black.
		The hands.
		The lungs.
		I remember that.

Looking Back

When I got out of prison,
Hoffa continues,
I began to feel my age,

more and more found
myself absent
-mindedly running

a hand over the only
map I had of it,
half reassurance,

half erosion, the
busted nose, scar
above the brow

written by a thug's blow
when I was the runt
on the block,

five o'clock shadow,
and something I
noticed just now,

a hole behind the right ear,
powder-scorched,
like Bobby Kennedy's,

where a slug,
and then the world,
passed right through.

The History Dept.

-No! Not the shrivel ray!

What's the matter with you, Mr. Hoffa?
There ain't no such thing as a shrivel ray.

Anybody seen the shrivel ray?

A Chorus Of One

Hoffa goes on:

I'd ridden in such processions before and doubtless would again. Or so I thought. I sat in a hearse beside a young priest still in his cassock from the funeral mass. I don't remember who the funeral was for. Maybe all of us. The priest laughed at the cars forced to nest in their exhaust by the curb as we passed. "They hate us." Then I noticed a hubcap propped against a tree. It looked familiar. You could say it opened my eyes to how I had changed. How we all had changed. The people. The nation. Our cars, the tread we're missing. Come to think of it, I never did ride in such a procession again, although I was given quite a few police escorts, except the time I really needed it.

Does this sound like singing, Walt?
Does it look like singing?
Our kind of singing?
Singing in our own words?
From the beginning
Hoffa has been singing to us
through his wooden mouth
about pride and striving and loss
and the emptiness that follows
them like an old man pushing

a broom through confetti
on New Year's Day.

Hoffa:

When I arrived I was alone. Not even accompanied by the
person I'd been. But the shades rose up, embraced me, and
elected me President of the International Brotherhood of
Man…

How the soil shifts
and groans. It's heard
this song before.
It knows what becomes
of every movement
however small
and can tell you
how fine print can be
and how all bargains
made with Management
end. And if you don't
believe its lesson
ask the marchers
in the tiny black hardhats,
demanding their pay.

After Words

A man goes into a bar. This happens over and over again. He decides to make the best of it. Henceforth, he says, this time will be called Happy Hour. Tonight everyone is there, the orphan and the amnesiac, the midget on the pogo stick, the opera singer and the duck (don't ask), why, even Jack Kennedy and Marilyn Monroe have come, fading into flashbulb gasps...

:

        Everyone but the ventriloquist,
        who prefers to drink alone.

About the Author

Bill Rector is a retired physician. He is former editor of the Yale Journal of Humanities in Medicine. His autobiographical poetry book, **bill,** was published in 2007 by Proem Press. **Biography of a Name** is the third chapbook to be published in the last few months. **Lost Moth,** about the sudden loss of his daughter, won the Epiphany Prize in 2017. **Two Worlds** will appear this summer from White Knuckle Press.

About the Press

Unsolicited Press is an independent publishing press based out of Northern California, Oregon, and Washington. We focus on literary fiction, creative nonfiction, and poetry. Learn more at www.unsolicitedpress.com

www.ingramcontent.com/pod-product-compliance
Lightning Source LLC
Chambersburg PA
CBHW062105270326
41931CB00013B/3222